MAKING Parents PROUD ★

A 4-week course to help junior highers build strong relationships with their parents

by Linda Heaner

Group
Loveland, Colorado

Making Parents Proud

Credits
Edited by Michael D. Warden
Cover designed by Jill Bendykowski and DeWain Stoll
Interior designed by Judy Atwood Bienick and Jan Aufdemberge
Cover photo by Brenda Rundback
Illustrations by Raymond Medici
Photo on p. 5 by Bob Taylor
Photo on p. 35 by Hildegard Adler

ISBN 1-55945-107-6
Printed in the United States of America

CONTENTS

MAKING PARENTS PROUD

MAKING PARENTS PROUD

"My friends put their parents down a lot. I really like my parents, but I don't want to seem like an odd- ball."

"My parents let me do whatever I want. I can go wherever I want any time—and I don't even need to tell them. Sometimes I wonder if they really care about me."

"I get along really well with my parents. I like doing things with them, and they're pretty easy to talk to. I don't ever want our relationship to change."

"I just wish my parents would try to understand me. I have so many questions I need answers to. I wish we could really talk with each other."

These comments from junior highers give glimpses of the wide range of relationships between kids and parents. Junior highers want and need positive relationships with their parents. According to Search Institute's study of early adolescents, 80 percent of young teenagers rate making parents proud as either very important or most important to them in their lives. Another recent study showed that junior highers want these three things from their parents:

● to be listened to;
● to be understood; and
● to have parents' total assurance of love and support no matter what kids do.

Middle school is a time of transition. No longer can kids be treated as children, yet they're not adults either. At this age, kids' minds are working overtime. They face conflict as they begin to question things they've always believed. They're on an exciting, yet sometimes discouraging, journey toward independence and maturity.

Nothing affects developing junior highers more than their family relationships. A family is a system. All relationships in a family are interconnected and each relationship affects the others.

In her book, *Traits of a Healthy Family* (Harper & Row), Dolores Curran cites 15 qualities healthy families possess. These qualities are listed in the box on page 5. Some kids have most of these traits in their families; some have only a few. But junior highers each need to know how to help develop these qualities in their family.

Middle schoolers each are at a different place in their relationship with their parents. This course will help equip junior highers with the skills they need to communicate more effectively with their parents and learn ways they can positively influence their home environment by changing how they communicate. Kids will learn how to build strong, positive relationships with their parents.

Traits of a Healthy Family

The healthy family . . .
- communicates and listens.
- affirms and supports each other.
- teaches respect for others.
- develops a sense of trust.
- has a sense of play and humor.
- exhibits a sense of shared responsibility.
- teaches a sense of right and wrong.
- has a strong sense of family in which rituals and traditions abound.
- has a balance of interaction among members.
- has a shared religious core.
- respects each other's privacy.
- values service to others.
- fosters table time and conversation.
- shares leisure time.
- admits to problems and seeks help for them.

COURSE OBJECTIVES

By the end of this course your students will:
- discover biblical building blocks to good communication with parents;
- improve their communication skills;
- learn how to earn their parents' trust;
- discover steps they can take to improve family relationships;
- understand the process of negotiating with parents; and
- learn different ways to show love to parents.

HOW TO USE THIS COURSE

ACTIVE LEARNING

Think back on an important lesson you've learned in life. Did you learn it from reading about it? from hearing about it? from something you experienced? Chances are, the most important lessons you've learned came from something you experienced. That's what active learning is—learning by doing. And active learning is a key element in Group's Active Bible Curriculum.

Active learning leads students in doing things that help them understand important principles, messages and ideas. It's a discovery process that helps kids internalize what they learn.

Each lesson section in Group's Active Bible Curriculum plays an important part in active learning:

The **Opener** involves kids in the topic in fun and unusual ways.

The **Action and Reflection** includes an experience designed to evoke specific feelings in the students. This section also processes those feelings through "How did you feel?" questions and applies the message to situations kids face.

The **Bible Application** actively connects the topic with the Bible. It helps kids see how the Bible is relevant to the situations they face.

The **Commitment** helps students internalize the Bible's message and commit to make changes in their lives.

The **Closing** funnels the lesson's message into a time of creative reflection and prayer.

When you put all the sections together, you get a lesson that's fun to teach—and kids get messages they'll remember.

BEFORE THE 4-WEEK SESSION

● Read the Introduction, the Course Objectives and This Course at a Glance.

● Decide how you'll publicize the course using the art on the Publicity Page (p. 9). Prepare fliers, newsletter articles and posters as needed.

● Look at the Bonus Ideas (p. 44) and decide which ones you'll use.

● Read the opening statements, Objectives and Bible Basis for the lesson. The Bible Basis shows how specific passages relate to junior highers today.

● Choose which Opener and Closing options to use. Each is appropriate for a different kind of group. The first option is often more active.

● Gather necessary supplies from This Lesson at a Glance.

● Read each section of the lesson. Adjust where necessary for your class size and meeting room.

BEFORE EACH LESSON

● The approximate minutes listed give you an idea of how long each activity will take. Each lesson is designed to take 35 to 60 minutes. Shorten or lengthen activities as needed to fit your group.

● If you see you're going to have extra time, do an activity or two from the "If You Still Have Time . . . " box or from the Bonus Ideas (p. 44).

● Dive into the activities with the kids. Don't be a spectator. The lesson will be more successful and rewarding to both you and your students.

● In this course, we often refer to "parents," though we don't mean to ignore single-parent families. We understand that many teenagers come from single-parent homes. If your class has kids from single-parent homes, be sensitive to adjust the wording to read "parent" as necessary.

HELPFUL HINTS

● The answers given after discussion questions are responses your students *might* give. They aren't the only answers or the "right" answers. If needed, use them to spark discussion. Kids won't always say what you wish they'd say. That's why some of the responses given are negative or controversial. If someone responds negatively, don't be shocked. Accept the person, and use the opportunity to explore other angles of the issue.

THIS COURSE AT A GLANCE

Before you dive into the lessons, familiarize yourself with each lesson aim. Then read the scripture passages.
- Study them as a background to the lessons.
- Use them as a basis for your personal devotions.
- Think about how they relate to kids' circumstances today.

LESSON 1: COMMUNICATING WITH PARENTS

Lesson Aim: To help junior highers identify the building blocks for good communication with their parents.

Bible Basis: Leviticus 19:3a; Ephesians 4:25, 29, 32; and 1 Peter 2:17.

LESSON 2: SPEAK FOR YOURSELF

Lesson Aim: To help junior highers learn to use "I" messages.

Bible Basis: Proverbs 12:18 and James 1:19.

LESSON 3: GAINING NEW FREEDOMS

Lesson Aim: To help junior highers discover specific ways they can increase parental trust and gain new freedoms.

Bible Basis: Proverbs 20:11 and Matthew 5:37.

LESSON 4: SHOWING LOVE

Lesson Aim: To help junior highers expand their ways of showing love to their parents.

Bible Basis: John 15:12 and Galatians 5:13b.

PUBLICITY PAGE

Grab your junior highers' attention! Copy this page, then cut and paste the art of your choice in your church bulletin or newsletter to advertise this course on parents. Or copy and use the ready-made flier as a bulletin insert. Permission to photocopy this clip art is granted for local church use.

Splash this art on posters, fliers or even postcards! Just add the vital details: the date and time the course begins, and where you'll meet.

It's that simple.

MAKING *Parents* PROUD ★

MAKING *Parents* PROUD ★

MAKING *Parents* PROUD ★

MAKING *Parents* PROUD ★

A 4-week junior high course on getting along with parents

Come to _____

On _____

At _____

Discover how to turn parents into friends!

COMMUNICATING WITH PARENTS

The junior high years mark the beginning of a new kind of a relationship with parents. As your young people develop better communication skills, they'll be able to build stronger, more positive relationships with their parents.

To help junior highers identify building blocks for good communication with their parents.

Students will:
- **compare communication to building a tower of blocks;**
- **discover positive communication building blocks in the Bible;**
- **discuss hindrances to positive communication; and**
- **evaluate their current communication with their parents.**

Look up the following scriptures. Then read the background paragraphs to see how the passages relate to your junior highers or middle schoolers.

In **Leviticus 19:3a**, the Lord commands through Moses that people must each respect their mother and father.

Families were very important in Old Testament times. In this passage, the writer reiterates this commandment as having particular importance.

Junior highers need to learn to respect their parents. Even when parents do something wrong or hurtful, kids can still respect parents for the position they hold as leaders of the family.

In **Ephesians 4:25, 29, 32**, Paul gives specific instructions about how God's people should relate to each other.

Paul's message in the verses helps spell out the lifestyle of a Christian. Here, he describes how honesty, encouragement and thoughtfulness are positive ways to build communication.

Junior highers live in a world of putdowns and criticism. But God's Word provides guidance to help kids build relationships with their parents rather than tear them down.

In **1 Peter 2:17**, Peter challenges the church to "show proper respect to everyone."

This passage reminds Christians that Earthly authorities should be respected and honored. Peter was concerned that Christians ought to obey the laws of government and families.

This passage emphasizes kids' need to respect those in positions of authority, even if kids don't agree with those people.

THIS LESSON AT A GLANCE

Section	Minutes	What Students Will Do	Supplies
Opener (Option 1)	5 to 10	**Easy or Hard**—Draw pictures of easy and hard things to talk about with parents.	Newsprint, markers
(Option 2)		**Take Your Pick**—Pick an image that's most like talking with parents.	
Action and Reflection	5 to 10	**Build Up or Break Down**—Try to build a tower of blocks.	"+ and - Cards" (p. 17), building blocks
Bible Application	15 to 20	**Find the Building Blocks**—Identify building blocks from the Bible for good communication.	Markers, newsprint, tape, Bibles, paper
Commitment	5 to 10	**How Am I Doing?**—Evaluate communication with parents.	"How Am I Doing?" handouts (p. 18), pencils
Closing (Option 1)	5 to 10	**Tennis Ball Toss**—Encourage each other by using a tennis ball.	Tennis ball
(Option 2)		**Here's What I See**—Tape communication affirmations to each other.	3×5 cards, tape, pencils

The Lesson

OPENER
(5 to 10 minutes)

☐ OPTION 1: EASY OR HARD

Copy the "Easy or Hard Chart" in the margin onto a sheet of newsprint. This chart will work even for kids who live with only one parent. Give kids each a marker. Say: **In each section of the chart, draw a picture that completes the open-ended sentence. For example, if it's easy to talk to your**

dad about homework, draw in the upper-righthand box a textbook, or a pen and paper.

When kids are finished, form a circle. Have kids each share their two "mom" drawings. Then have kids each share their two "dad" drawings.

Ask:

● **Was this activity easy or hard? Why or why not?**

● **Is it easier to talk with Mom or Dad about most things? Explain.**

● **What would you like to talk about more often with your parents?** (Friend problems; schoolwork.)

Say: **Communicating with parents isn't always easy. But it is important. Today we're going to examine how good communication can help build positive relatonships with parents.**

Easy or Hard Chart	
It's easy to talk with my mom about . . .	It's easy to talk with my dad about . . .
It's hard to talk with my mom about . . .	It's hard to talk with my dad about . . .

☐ OPTION 2: TAKE YOUR PICK

Number three corners of the room #1, #2 and #3. Read aloud the "Corner Statements" below. Read each statement set once for "Mom," then again for "Dad." For each set of choices, have kids go to the corner that best reflects their response, then answer these questions in their groups:

● **Why did you choose this corner?** (We're always tossing ideas around; we never really talk.)

● **Did you choose the same answers for your dad and mom? Why or why not?** (I can talk easier with one; I talk to both the same.)

After everyone is finished, ask:

● **What did you like about this activity?** (The comparisons were fun; it made me think about my family.)

Corner Statements
Talking with my mom is most like . . .
Talking with my dad is most like . . .

	Set #1	Set #2	Set #3
Corner #1:	a tennis match	a cold war	a garden
Corner #2:	a silent movie	a trial	a desert
Corner #3:	a boxing match	a fireside chat	a land mine

● **What did you dislike about this activity?** (It was hard to decide between some items; I felt uncomfortable sharing about my family with other kids.)

Say: **Sometimes talking with parents may seem more like a battle than a relationship. We all go through times when communication is difficult or strained. Yet we know** good communication is critical to a healthy relationship with parents. Today we'll discover why.

BUILD UP OR BREAK DOWN

Form groups of four. Give groups each 20 "+" cards and 10 "-" cards from the "+ and - Cards" (p. 17), and 20 blocks. Blocks can be wooden, cardboard or plastic. Have groups each shuffle their cards.

Say: **In your group, use the cards to build a block tower. The rules are simple: Going clockwise, take turns drawing a card. If you draw a "+" card, add a block to the tower. If you draw a "-" card, take a block away from the tower. If you draw a "-" card first, just keep drawing until you draw a "+" card. You have one minute.**

Call time before any group goes through all the cards. Then have groups compare towers.

Ask:

● **How did you feel while building your tower?** (Discouraged; anxious.)

● **How did you feel when you got a "-" card?** (Angry; disappointed.)

● **Did you work well with other group members? Why or why not?** (No, I wanted to build the tower differently; yes, we worked as a team.)

● **How is building a tower like communicating with your parents?** (It takes time for it to be established; every part of the tower is important—so everything you say is important.)

● **How is a "-" card like bad communication with parents?** (It takes away what's already been built; it hurts the relationship.)

Say: **You can say things that help and build up others, or you can tear them down with your words. Let's look at several building blocks for positive communication with your parents.**

FIND THE BUILDING BLOCKS

Say: **God's Word gives many helpful guidelines or building blocks for good communication.**

Write Ephesians 4:25 on a sheet of newsprint, and tape the newsprint to the wall. Read aloud the verse, then ask:

● **What building blocks in this verse do you see for good communication?** (Don't lie; we belong to each other.)

● **How could we sum up this verse in one word or phrase?** (Tell the truth; be united.)

Form five groups. A group can be one person. Give each kid a Bible, and assign each group a different verse from the following: Leviticus 19:3a; Ephesians 4:25; Ephesians 4:29; Ephesians 4:32; and 1 Peter 2:17. Give groups each several sheets of paper and a marker.

Say: **Read your assigned verse. Then pick out key words,**

phrases or themes about good communication. Write one key word, phrase or theme on each sheet of paper. Then tear your paper to form building-block shapes.

When groups are finished, have them each explain what they wrote. Then have groups tape their paper building blocks to the wall to form one large tower.

Call everyone together, and distribute more paper. Have kids brainstorm words and phrases that mean the opposite of the building-block words they taped to the wall. As kids share, have volunteers write each response on a separate sheet of paper, then tear each sheet of paper to form a dynamite-blast shape. Then have volunteers tape the dynamite-blast shapes on top of the paper building-block tower.

Ask:

● **How do these "communication blasters" hurt relationships?** (They break down trust; they make people angry.)

● **How does always being honest affect your relationship with your parents?** (They know they can trust me; it doesn't do any good.)

● **How does lying affect your relationship with your parents?** (They're always suspicious; they get mad.)

HOW AM I DOING?

Say: **You can't control whether your parents will use these positive building blocks. But you can decide to always follow them personally.**

Give kids each a "How Am I Doing?" handout (p. 18) and a pencil. Have kids each complete all of the handout except the Commitment Box. When everyone is finished, ask:

● **What have you learned about yourself by filling out this handout?** (I do more positive things than negative; I don't think about my parents much.)

● **Which letter in the left column did you score highest on? Why did you score highest on that one?**

Say: **Now complete the Commitment Box at the bottom of your handout. Choose one of the suggestions listed, or create your own—as long as it's specific.**

Have kids each share their commitment with the group.

COMMITMENT
(5 to 10 minutes)

Table Talk

The Table Talk activity in this course helps junior highers and middle schoolers discuss family communication with their parents.

If you choose to use the Table Talk activity, this is a good time to show students the "Table Talk" handout (p. 19). Ask them each to spend time with their parents completing it.

Before kids leave, give them each the "Table Talk" handout to take home, or tell them you'll be sending it to their parents.

Or use the Table Talk idea found in the Bonus Ideas (p. 44) for a meeting based on the handout.

C L O S I N G
(5 to 10 minutes)

☐ OPTION 1: TENNIS BALL TOSS

Have kids stand in a circle. Hold up a tennis ball.

Say: **Each of you uses good communication building blocks every day. Let's use this tennis ball to recognize those skills. I'll think of someone in the circle who has a good communication skill. Without naming the person, I'll describe his or her skill, such as he or she is honest, then bounce the ball to him or her. Then that person will say something positive about someone else in the circle, then pass the ball to him or her. We'll continue until everyone has held the ball at least once.**

After naming the communication skill you see in one of the kids, bounce the ball to him or her. Encourage kids to bounce the ball to somebody new each time. After everyone has held the ball at least once, close with prayer, thanking God for his special gifts of communication and for kids' parents.

☐ OPTION 2: HERE'S WHAT I SEE

Form a circle. Give kids each five 3×5 cards, tape and a pencil. Say: **Each of us has special communication skills given by God. On each of your 3×5 cards write one good communication skill you see in each of the five people to your right. You might write that someone is a good listener or has a loving attitude. After writing your cards, tape them each to the appropriate person.**

When everyone is finished, say: **Take your cards home as reminders to use your good communication skills with your parents.**

Close with prayer, thanking God for kids' special communication skills and for their parents.

If You Still Have Time . . .

Human Building Blocks—Have students work together to build a human tower. After everyone is in place, say: **Just as you have an important role in holding the tower together, so you have an important role in building strong relationships with your parents.**

Have kids each sit on the floor, and ask:

● **What would've happened if I'd pulled someone from the center of the tower?** (It would've collapsed; it would've fallen.)

● **What would happen if you "pulled out" of building relationships with your parents?** (The relationship would fail; my mom wouldn't talk to me.)

Thumbs Up, Thumbs Down—Form a circle, and have kids give a "thumbs up" or a "thumbs down" according to whether they agree with each item you'll read below:

● **My parents understand how I feel about . . . (school, friends, chores, money, peer pressure, house rules, clothes, grades, my future, God, privacy, sex, dating, music, hairstyles)**

After going through the list, ask:

● **How can you work to improve the openness in your relationship with your parents?** (Tell them how I feel; ask their advice.)

✚ AND ▨ CARDS

Photocopy and cut apart these cards to use in the Build Up or Break Down activity.

HOW AM I DOING?

Rank each statement below from 1 to 5 (1= almost never; 5= almost always) to see how you build up or tear down your family relationships.

I build up communication with my parents by:	I break down communication with my parents by:
____ a. telling my parents I appreciate them.	____ a. smart-mouthing.
____ b. sharing my feelings.	____ b. stuffing my feelings inside.
____ c. talking to them about what's important to me.	____ c. pretending not to hear.
____ d. speaking to my parents in a respectful way.	____ d. not looking at them.
____ e. listening when my parents talk.	____ e. being critical of them.
____ f. apologizing when I'm wrong.	____ f. acting like I know it all.
____ g. telling the truth even when it's hard.	____ g. refusing to listen to my parents' viewpoint.
____ h. laughing and having fun with my parents.	____ h. blaming or accusing them.
____ i. forgiving my parents' mistakes.	____ i. purposely disobeying them.

Score Card

Count the number of checks you have in each column. Then rate your relationship-building skills based on the scale below.

● **6 to 9 more communication-builders than communication breakers**—You're a communicating dynamo! Keep up the good work.

● **3 to 5 more communication-builders than communication breakers**—You have satisfactory communication skills. But you could work on reducing the number of communication breakers in your family relationships.

● **1 to 2 more communication-builders than communication breakers**—You came out on the positive side—but just barely. When it comes to family communication skills, you're treading on dangerous ground.

● **Same number of communication-builders and communication breakers**—You have an inconsistent communication style. Your parents probably don't know how you'll respond from one situation to the next. Work on building up your positive communication skills and avoiding communication breakers.

● **More communication breakers than communication-builders**—Yikes! You may be damaging your family relationships. Start today to practice positive communication skills and follow the communication advice in this lesson.

Commitment Box

Place a check beside the things you'll commit to do this week.

To build positive communication with my parents, I will:
____ say one encouraging thing each day to my mom or dad.
____ speak to my parents in a respectful way.
____ talk to my parents about my problems.
____ be honest with my parents.
____ other: _____.
____ other: _____.

Table Talk

To the Parent: We're talking at church about ways to strengthen relationships with parents. Use the suggestions below to deepen your relationship with your junior higher. Enjoy getting to know each other.

Name Game

Each of you write the first name of your parent or junior higher down the left side of a sheet of paper. Next to each letter of the name, write a word starting with that letter that describes that person in a positive way. Share your descriptions.

Parent

● Tell your junior higher a "when I was a teenager" story.

● Plan a time this month to do something special with your middle schooler, such as go to a movie, go out to eat or go bowling.

Complete the following statements:

● The hardest thing about being a parent for me is . . .

● When I was growing up, I disagreed most with my parents about . . .

—friends	—chores	—makeup
—clothes	—curfew	—grades
—dating	—other: _____	

● Something I really wanted to do when I was growing up, but my parents wouldn't let me was . . .

Junior Higher

● Tell a "someday, when I'm a parent" story.

● Do something with your parent you ordinarily don't do together, such as fix a meal, wash the car or go grocery shopping.

Complete the following statements:

● The greatest strength of our family is . . .

● If I could get rid of one family rule, it'd be . . .

● The hardest thing about being a junior higher today is . . .

Family Quiz

Have family members each write endings to the following open-ended statements. When everyone is finished, share what you wrote.

● My favorite family holiday is . . .

● A special memory of growing up was when . . .

● Something I'd really like to do but haven't done yet is . . .

● I show my parent/junior higher I love him or her by . . .

● I feel loved by my parent/junior higher when . . .

Think of someone you admire or want to be like. Without identifying the person, write three qualities that really stand out in that person. See if your parent or junior higher can guess who you chose. Then identify your person.

Think of one quality you admire or respect in your parent or junior higher. Tell him or her what it is.

Together, read Ephesians 4:25-32. Talk about how you can show these qualities in your relationships.

Family Projects

1. Set up a weekly or monthly family council meeting. Gather the whole family together to talk about positive and negative things that have happened, to discuss family rules or plan family activities.

2. Use Post-It Notes to express thanks to each other for doing ordinary jobs around the house.

3. Design a holiday just for your family. Decide what to call it and what date it will fall on each year or month. Design a family banner to be hung on that holiday. Brainstorm ideas for how you'll celebrate your unique day together.

LESSON 2

SPEAK FOR YOURSELF

Communication between junior highers and their parents can often become garbled and misunderstood. Students will learn how to more clearly communicate their thoughts, feelings and needs by using "I" messages.

LESSON AIM

To help junior highers learn to use "I" messages.

OBJECTIVES

Students will:
- discuss how people see the same things in different ways;
- discover the importance of listening to others;
- learn to use "I" messages; and
- commit to use "I" messages with their parents for a week.

BIBLE BASIS
PROVERBS 12:18
JAMES 1:19

Look up the following scriptures. Then read the background paragraphs to see how the passages relate to your junior highers or middle schoolers.

In **Proverbs 12:18**, the writer emphasizes the impact words can have on other people.

The author clearly understood the negative impact words could have on someone. Words *can* hurt. But the author also knew people could use words to heal.

Junior highers sometimes speak carelessly. They're sometimes unaware how their words and tone of voice affect their parents. These verses encourage kids to use encouraging words rather than destructive ones.

In **James 1:19**, the Apostle James says to be "quick to listen" and "slow to become angry." James emphasizes that listening is an essential part of good communication. Our tendency is just the opposite—to be quick to talk and slow to listen.

Middle schoolers want others to understand and listen to them. Parents want that too. By developing the habit of listening and thinking before speaking, kids can greatly improve communication with parents.

THIS LESSON AT A GLANCE

Section	Minutes	What Students Will Do	Supplies
Opener (Option 1)	5 to 10	**Pick One**—Pick an object to describe their relationship with their parents.	Various objects
(Option 2)		**Agree or Disagree**—Identify things they and their parents agree or disagree on.	Tape, newsprint, markers
Action and Reflection	5 to 10	**Squares**—Count how many squares they see in a picture.	Poster of 16 equal-size squares
Bible Application	10 to 20	**Stop, Look and Listen**—Learn to listen and use "I" messages.	Bible, thread, newsprint, "I Say, I Say" handouts (p. 26), pencils
Commitment	10 to 15	**What'd You Say?**—Commit to use "I" messages this week.	"I Say, I Say" handouts from Stop, Look and Listen, pencils
Closing (Option 1)	up to 5	**Special Notes**—Make card affirmations for each other.	3×5 cards, pencils, tape
(Option 2)		**Circle Messages**—Give an affirming "I" message to another person.	

The Lesson

☐ OPTION 1: PICK ONE

Form a circle. Lay the objects from the following list (or others you pick yourself) in the middle of the circle. Say: **Pick the object that best represents your relationship with your parents. Then explain why you picked the object you did. It's okay if someone takes the object you choose. Just get it from that person when it's your turn.**

Here's a list of suggested objects and possible reasons for picking them:
- matches—explosive relationship;
- sandpaper—rub each other the wrong way;
- mitten—warm, protective;
- pencil—able to correct mistakes;

● Ace bandage—support each other;

● glue—tight bonds between family members;

● Kleenex—make each other cry;

● Band-Aid—cover up serious problems;

● scissors—always make cutting remarks against each other; and

● stuffed animal—comfortable, but we don't talk much.

After kids have each explained their object, point out how some chose the same object but for different reasons. Say: **Just as some of you saw the same objects in different ways, so you and your parents can see the same situations from different perspectives. So when you disagree with your parents, that doesn't mean one of you is wrong. It's often just a matter of perspective.**

☐ OPTION 2: AGREE OR DISAGREE

Tape two sheets of newsprint to a wall. Use a marker to write these sentences each on a separate sheet of newsprint:

● One thing my parents and I agree on is . . .

● One thing my parents and I disagree on is . . .

Give kids each a marker, and have kids write their responses on the appropriate newsprint. Discuss kids' responses, then say: **You and your parents don't always see things the same way.**

Table Talk Follow-Up

If you sent the "Table Talk" handout (p. 19) to parents last week, discuss students' reactions to the activity. Ask volunteers to share what they learned from the discussion with their parents.

ACTION AND REFLECTION

(5 to 10 minutes)

Poster Diagram

SQUARES

Before the lesson, make a poster of 16 equal-size squares (see "Poster Diagram" in the margin).

Say: **Let's see how we can each look at the same thing and see it differently. I'm going to show you something and ask you a question. A few seconds later I'll ask each of you for an answer. Don't speak until I call on you.**

Show the poster for about 10 seconds. Then turn the poster around and ask:

● **How many squares did you see?**

Have kids each give their answer, then turn the poster back around. If kids consistently say "16," have them look more closely. If kids include the outer square, or any of the squares produced by grouping four to nine squares together—

they'll answer with a number higher than 16. If necessary, give kids a clue about how to see more squares. After kids have each answered, ask:

● **How'd you feel when others answered differently from you?** (Defensive; worried that my answer might be wrong.)

● **Did you want to change your answer after someone else responded differently? Why or why not?** (Yes, because I wasn't sure of my answer; no, because I would've felt like I was cheating.)

● **How is it possible to look at the same picture and see it differently?** (By focusing on different parts of the poster; by not really looking at it closely.)

Say: **When you see something differently from others, you have a choice to make. You can see only what you want to see, or you can let others show you what they see.**

Hold up the poster again, and ask volunteers to point out squares they see. Say: **Many arguments occur because we don't really try to see the other person's point of view.**

Ask:

● **How might this discussion apply to your relationship with your parents?** (A lot of our fights begin because we don't listen to each other; my parents don't try to understand my point of view.)

● **How might your relationship change if you both really tried to see the other's point of view?** (We wouldn't fight as much; I'd understand my parents' motives better.)

Say: **God wants our relationships to work. In the Bible, we can find helpful advice to know how to make them work.**

STOP, LOOK AND LISTEN

Form groups of three or four. Give groups each a Bible and 10 to 20 pieces of thread. Assign groups each one of the following verses: Proverbs 12:18 or James 1:19. Have groups each read their verse and pick out words or phrases that describe positive messages they can give others. Have groups twist together a piece of thread for each word or phrase they pick out. Then have kids each try to break the bundle of threads with their hands.

Call everyone together, and ask:

● **Why couldn't you break your threads?** (They were too strong banded together; the bundle was too thick.)

● **How are the threads like positive communication?** (They reinforce each other; just using a few doesn't help as much as using them all.)

● **How do you feel when someone really listens to you?** (Closer to him or her; understood.)

● **How can you tell when someone is really listening to you?** (He looks interested; she ask questions.)

Say: **When we listen, we tell others we're interested in them and think what they feel is important. Listening is**

BIBLE
APPLICATION
(10 to 20 minutes)

one of the most important communication skills.

There's one more skill that's vital for good communication.

On a sheet of newsprint, copy the "I Chart" from the margin. Using the information on the newsprint, point out the differences between the two kinds of messages. Say: **With an "I" message, I take responsibility for building communication by speaking for myself only, rather than blaming someone else. Here are some examples:**

Ask:

● **How do you feel when I say, "I need you to be quiet and listen"?** (Okay, I'll try to quiet down; I understand it's important to you.)

● **How do you feel when I say, "You're always talking! Be quiet!"?** (Angry; accused.)

Say: **"I" messages help us talk about a person's actions without making the person feel attacked. Let's do a handout to help us apply "I" messages to "you" messages we hear every day.**

Give kids each an "I Say, I Say" handout (p. 26) and a pencil. Point out the "I" message definition, then have kids each look at the first example in the first section: "Stay out of my room."

Ask:

● **How could you say this with an "I" message?** (I feel invaded when you come into my room uninvited; I want to be in my room by myself.)

Have kids each look at the first example in the second section: "Clean your room."

Ask:

● **How could you respond to this with an "I" statement?** (I feel angry when you tell me how and when to do things; I think it's clean.)

Form pairs, and have kids each complete the handout except for the Commitment Box. Have kids each share their responses with their partner.

Call everyone together, and have volunteers from each pair share one thing they wrote. Then say: **We've practiced using "I" messages in everyday situations. Let's carry on our practice by committing to use "I" messages this coming week.**

I Chart

"I" Messages	"You" Messages
● Speak only for myself	● Speak only about you
● Use "I think," "I feel," "I need"	● Use "You always," "You never," "You should"
● Place no blame	● Blame the other person
● Respect the other person	● Degrade the other person
● Help others respond without anger	● Make others defensive so they don't hear

---

COMMITMENT
(10 to 15 minutes)

WHAT'D YOU SAY?

Have kids brainstorm common situations they face every week and how they could use "I" messages in those situations. For example, when people receive failing grades they don't agree with, instead of saying, "The teacher failed me," they could go to their teacher and say, "I feel the grade is unfair."

After several kids have shared, have kids each complete the Commitment Box at the bottom of their handout and tear off the box. Have kids each take their Commitment Box home as a reminder to use "I" messages this coming week.

☐ OPTION 1: SPECIAL NOTES

Form a circle. Give kids each three 3×5 cards and a pencil. Have kids each fold their 3×5 cards to form a little greeting-card shape. Say: **Write your name on the front of each card, then toss your cards into a pile in the circle.**

When everyone is finished, have kids each draw from the pile three new cards of three different people.

Say: **Inside each card, write one positive "I" message for each of the three people listed on your cards. Start your "I" messages with, "I'm happy when I'm around you because . . . " or "I feel good about knowing you because . . . "**

Give kids each three strips of tape, and have them each tape their cards to the wall. Allow kids a few minutes to read all the cards. Leave the cards up until the end of the fourth session. Then let kids each take their cards home.

Close with prayer, thanking God for making everyone unique and valuable.

☐ OPTION 2: CIRCLE MESSAGES

Form a circle. Say: **Now that we've committed to use "I" messages, let's start by using them with each other.**

Have kids each give a positive "I" message to the person on their right by using one of these beginnings:
- I think you're special because . . .
- I feel happy when I'm around you because . . .

After everyone has shared an "I" message, pray: **Thanks, Lord, for making us each special. Help us serve you as the unique people we are. In Jesus' name, amen.**

CLOSING
(up to 5 minutes)

If You Still Have Time . . .

Non-Verbal Guess—Have one junior higher pick out a word on the "I Say, I Say" Feeling Words list and act it out non-verbally while the rest of the group tries to guess the word. Have kids take turns acting out words.

Point of View—Randomly point to things in your meeting room, such as a wall, poster, light, Bible, chair or door. As you point to each object, ask:
- **Do you like it? Why or why not?**

Point out how different people had different opinions of the objects in the room.
Ask:
- **Is an object "wrong" just because someone doesn't like it? Why or why not?** (No, it's a matter of opinion; yes, everyone would like it if there was nothing wrong with it.)
- **Are your parents wrong just because they disagree with you? Why or why not?** (Yes, usually; my parents don't understand me; no, sometimes I'm wrong; sometimes neither of us is wrong.)

I SAY, I SAY

Complete this handout to help learn to use "I" messages in everyday situations. Read the "I" message definition and the list of Feeling Words to help you write responses to the statements below.

| **"I" Message**—saying in a respectful way what I think, how I feel or what I need |

Feeling Words

- worried
- 10-feet tall
- small
- proud
- exhausted
- excited
- sad

- angry
- stepped on
- confused
- confident
- bored
- surprised
- hopeful

- hurt
- happy
- frustrated
- discouraged
- invaded
- silly
- rejected

Change the following "you" messages to "I" messages.

1. Stay out of my room.

2. You're always telling me what to do.

3. My math teacher is no good.

4. Don't treat me like dirt.

5. My brother is a real geek.

6. You're never ready on time.

7. Get off my back.

Respond with "I" messages to these questions and statements from parents.

1. Clean your room.

2. How was school today?

3. You're supposed to be doing the dishes—not watching television.

4. You look angry. What's wrong?

5. You'll never pass that test if you study with that music on.

6. What's taking you so long? Hurry up in there!

Commitment Box

This week I'll:
- try to use "I" messages each day with my parents.
- speak in a respectful voice to my parents.
- listen to what my parents are saying.
- show respect for my parent's point of view.

Signed _____

GAINING NEW FREEDOMS

Gaining independence from parents is a gradual process; it doesn't happen overnight. Parents often even resist giving independence because they care about their kids and want to protect them. But there are positive steps junior highers can take to make that transition easier.

To help junior highers discover specific ways they can increase parental trust and gain new freedoms.

Students will:
● **compare breaking out of a circle with gaining independence from parents;**
● **discover biblical principles for dealing with conflict;**
● **learn to negotiate with parents when conflicts arise; and**
● **discuss ways to earn more freedom from their parents.**

Look up the following scriptures. Then read the background paragraphs to see how the passages relate to your junior highers or middle schoolers.

In **Proverbs 20:11**, the writer says people's hearts are shaped by their deeds.

In this passage, the author claims that the activities people choose when young will determine the kind of people they become. At the same time, the author reaffirms a time-tested truth: Actions speak louder than words.

Junior highers each will find that their actions tell the kind of person they are. Kids' actions can either increase their parents' trust and respect for them or teach parents that their kids can't be trusted.

In **Matthew 5:37**, Jesus talks about making oaths.

LESSON AIM

OBJECTIVES

BIBLE BASIS
PROVERBS 20:11
MATTHEW 5:37

The people were swearing by heaven or Earth or the city of Jerusalem to give added impact to their oaths. Jesus says that our word alone should be enough.

Junior highers must realize the importance of their "yes" or "no." Being people of their word only comes with practice in doing what they say they'll do.

THIS LESSON AT A GLANCE

Section	Minutes	What Students Will Do	Supplies
Opener (Option 1)	up to 5	**What Do You Want?**—Check what they want most from their parents.	"What Do You Want?" handouts (p. 34), pencils, tape, newsprint, marker
(Option 2)		**Conflict in My House**—Rate areas of family conflict.	Tape, newsprint, marker
Action and Reflection	10 to 20	**Break Out**—Try to break out of a circle of peers.	
Bible Application	5 to 10	**Do You Promise?**—Look at what the Bible says about keeping our word.	Bibles, newsprint, markers
Commitment	10 to 20	**What Can I Do?**—Find ways to negotiate and gain new freedoms.	"What Can I Do?" handouts (p. 35), pencils
Closing (Option 1)	up to 5	**You Can Count on Me**—Write how other group members are dependable.	3×5 cards, pencils
(Option 2)		**Paired Honesty**—Tell partners honest things they like about each other.	

The Lesson

OPENER
(up to 5 minutes)

☐ OPTION 1: WHAT DO YOU WANT?

Give kids each a "What Do You Want?" handout (p. 34) and a pencil. Have kids each complete their handout. Tape a sheet of newsprint to the wall, and number it from 1 to 20.

When everyone is finished, gather kids around the newsprint. For each item on the handout, ask:
● **How many of you chose this as one of your top five?**

Tally the votes for each item and write the results next to the appropriate number on the newsprint. Have kids each star the item on their list that's most important to them. While they do that, circle the five highest scoring answers for the whole group.

Ask:

● **How many have one of your five answers in the top five for the group?**

● **How many have a starred answer in the group's top five?**

Ask for volunteers to share their starred answer.

Ask:

● **Why do so many of us have similar answers?** (We have the same problems at home; all parents are the same.)

● **How would you feel talking to your parents about your needs?** (I have; I'd feel awkward.)

☐ OPTION 2: CONFLICT IN MY HOUSE

Tape a sheet of newsprint to the wall. On the newsprint, copy the "Rating Instructions" from the box in the margin. Say: **I'm going to read a series of things you and your parents might disagree about. Rate how much conflict each item causes in your home, following the instructions on the newsprint.**

Read aloud these items, pausing briefly after each one to allow kids to respond:

● **Television**
● **Chores**
● **Choice of friends**
● **Money**
● **Privacy**
● **Telephone use**
● **Free-time activities**
● **Curfew**
● **Parental expectations**
● **Clothing**
● **Grades**
● **Family time**
● **Homework**
● **Music**

Ask:

● **What surprised you about this activity?** (Other families deal with different issues than mine; a lot of people argue over clothes.)

● **How do you feel when you and your parents fight?** (Angry; I feel like just walking away.)

● **How can conflicts hurt your family?** (We say things we don't mean; it's hard to open up to your parents after a fight.)

● **How can conflicts help your family?** (We work things out; they really get to hear my side.)

> ### Rating Instructions
> ● No conflict—sit on the floor.
> ● Small conflict—squat down.
> ● Medium conflict—kneel on one knee.
> ● Large conflict—stand up.
> ● Huge conflict—stand up and wave your arms.

BREAK OUT

Say: **Conflicts happen when you and your parents disagree about the rules and boundaries you should live within. Let's have some fun with boundaries.**

Have two-thirds of your kids form one group and the other third form another group. Give groups their instructions separately.

To the larger group, say: **Form a circle around the smaller group. Join hands around them. Your job is to make sure the inner group stays inside the circle. If the group tries to get out, work together to keep it in.**

To the smaller group, say: **Let the other group make a**

ACTION AND REFLECTION
(10 to 20 minutes)

circle around you. Then try to break out of the circle any way you can. You're responsible only for yourself. If you get out, you can cheer the others on, but don't help them.

Play the game for one or two minutes. Then call everyone together and ask the larger group:

● **How'd you feel when those inside began trying to get out?** (Suspicious; afraid they'd try to get out through me.)

● **How'd you feel when they kept trying to get out?** (Angry; defiant.)

● **What physical changes took place in the outer group as the game went on?** (We linked arms; we pushed against the other kids.)

Ask the smaller group:

● **What were you feeling as you tried to escape?** (I wanted to wait for the right moment; I was hesitant.)

● **How'd you feel when it wasn't so easy to get out?** (I thought I'd get out no matter what; I was ready to give up.)

● **How'd you feel about those in the outer circle?** (Playful; frustrated.)

● **How is this like trying to break out of your parent's restrictions?** (I get frustrated with them; I feel caged.)

Play a second game using the same groups. Again, give instructions separately. To the larger group, say: **Form a circle around the other kids just as before. Keep the smaller group inside your boundaries.**

To the smaller group, say: **Stay inside the circle this time. Act curious, looking out and near the edge, but don't break out of the circle.**

Have kids play for about 30 seconds. Then call everyone together, and ask:

● **What feelings did you have this time?** (I was more relaxed; I kept expecting them to try something.)

● **What made the two games so different?** (The inner group didn't act the same; it was boring because there was no resistance.)

● **How did you feel about the other group?** (Less hostile; I was still suspicious.)

● **How is this like what happens when you stay within the boundaries your parents set?** (More peaceful; no conflict.)

● **How is it different?** (My parents want to protect me, but this game just tries to keep me caged; my parents' boundaries aren't as clear as these.)

BIBLE APPLICATION
(5 to 10 minutes)

DO YOU PROMISE?

Say: **We've seen how handling conflict can affect your relationship with your parents. Let's look in the Bible to see how trust plays a part in those conflicts.**

Give kids each a Bible. Form groups of five or fewer. Assign groups either Proverbs 20:11 or Matthew 5:37. Have groups each think of a phrase or sentence that summarizes the verse's meaning. For example, for Proverbs 20:11, kids might say, "Actions speak louder than words" or "Your behavior says a lot about you." For Matthew 5:37, kids might say, "Keep your word" or "Tell the truth."

Give groups each a sheet of newsprint and a marker. Have groups each draw a picture or symbol that represents their summary statement. When groups have finished, have them try to guess what each group's summary statement is.

After all the summary statements have been discovered, ask:

● **What do these verses have to do with trust?** (If people do what they say, you trust them; it's easier to trust an honest person.)

● **How does trust relate to the circle games we played earlier?** (You have to trust your teammate to help you keep someone in the circle; you couldn't trust the people inside the circle.)

● **What part does trust play in gaining independence from your parents?** (You can't trick your parents and expect them to trust you; you need to trust their ability to know how much independence you can handle.)

● **Why do parents set up boundaries on your freedom?** (They want to protect you; they know what you can handle.)

● **Should boundaries be the same for all kids? Explain.** (Yes, that way everything is fair; no, because different kids have different needs and problems.)

● **How do parents know when it's time to remove some of the boundaries they've set?** (When you prove you can handle new things; when you take on more responsibility for yourself.)

Say: **Gaining independence from your parents is a gradual process. Much of it depends on your words and actions. The way you act and react will either increase your parents' trust and respect for you, or teach them to not trust you.**

Have volunteers give examples of how their words and actions can help parents trust them more. For example, be honest, do what you say you'll do, ask for their advice.

Say: **The best way to gain more freedom is to show you keep your word and are dependable.**

WHAT CAN I DO?

Say: **Let's look at practical ways we can apply what we just learned.**

Give kids each a "What Can I Do?" handout (p. 35) and a pencil. Review with kids the Negotiating With Parents box from the handout. Say: **Step #1 shows respect and understanding for others. Step #2 lets parents know how you think and feel. Step #3 helps your family figure out what the real conflict is about. It may be beneath the surface issue. Step #4 tries to choose the best solution from**

COMMITMENT
(10 to 20 minutes)

several alternatives you've discussed.

Instruct groups each to refer to the steps often as they do this activity. Form pairs. Assign each pair one of the role plays in Part 1 of the handout. Have pairs assign parts and prepare a short role play using the negotiating steps on the handout.

When pairs are ready, have each role-play their situation. After each role play, ask:

- **What was good about this role play?**
- **What did you dislike about this role play?**
- **How is this role play like your situation at home?**
- **How is it different?**
- **What else could be done to resolve this conflict more easily?**

Have pairs each choose a situation from Part 2 of the handout and devise a plan to earn the freedom written there. For example, pairs that choose situation #1 must each devise a plan they can follow in cooperation with their parents to gain the freedom to stay out later during the week. The only rule is that each plan must involve talking with parents.

When everyone is finished, have pairs each explain their plan to the group. After everyone has shared, ask:

- **What are other freedoms you'd like to gain from your parents?**
- **How do you know you're ready to have that freedom?**
- **How could you go about gaining those freedoms?**

Say: **Choose one freedom you'd like to gain, and complete the Commitment Box on your handout to start you on your way to gaining that freedom.**

When kids have each completed their Commitment Box, say: **Tear off your Commitment Box, and take it home with you. Display it in a prominent place in your house to remind you of your goal.**

CLOSING
(up to 5 minutes)

☐ OPTION 1: YOU CAN COUNT ON ME

Form a circle. Give kids each four 3×5 cards and a pencil. On separate cards, have kids each write a way four different group members demonstrate dependability. For example, kids might write that a person keeps his or her word, or that he or she is always on time. Have kids each write a card for the two people to their right and the two people to their left. When everyone is finished, have kids each read their cards aloud and give them to the appropriate people.

Lead a closing prayer, thanking God for the power to be dependable and work out conflicts in families.

☐ OPTION 2: PAIRED HONESTY

Form pairs, and have partners stand facing each other. Say: **Practice your honesty skills by telling your partner one thing you really like about him or her. When I say,**

"Switch," find a new partner and tell that person one thing you really like about him or her. We'll continue through four or five switches.

Call "switch" every 15 seconds. Continue until kids have had four or five partners.

Gather everyone in a circle and close with prayer, thanking God for the strength to be honest and the ability to resolve conflicts in families.

If You Still Have Time . . .

Responsibility and Privilege—Have kids each complete these statements:
- One responsibility I have at home is . . .
- One privilege I've recently gained is . . .
- One responsibility I plan to take on this year is . . .
- One added privilege I hope to gain this year is . . .

Newsletter Report—Have kids compile the results of the group's "What Do You Want?" handouts to determine kids' top five responses. Write the results along with a brief explanation of what kids are learning in Sunday school. Include your report in the next church newsletter.

Role Play—Role-play situations from the "What Can I Do?" handout (p. 35) that weren't done earlier. Or have kids create a problem situation to role-play. After the role play, ask the discussion questions that follow the role plays from the What Can I Do? activity (p. 31).

What do you want?

What do you want most from your parents? Check five answers.

I want my parents to . . .

1. _____listen to me.

2. _____give me permission to do what I want.

3. _____assure me of their love.

4. _____let me grow up.

5. _____allow me to question their values and decisions.

6. _____be more flexible.

7. _____let me express myself.

8. _____help me make decisions.

9. _____give me money.

10. _____spend time with me.

11. _____give me freedom to make more choices myself.

12. _____forgive my mistakes.

13. _____be interested in me as a person.

14. _____not put so many restrictions on me.

15. _____think I'm someone special.

16. _____be more lighthearted and fun.

17. _____respect me.

18. _____support me in decisions I make.

19. _____be willing to change rules as I get older.

20. _____trust me.

What Can I Do?

Part 1—Role-play these situations using the steps from the Negotiating With Parents box.
1. You want to watch a certain TV show; your parent wants you to do your homework.
2. Your mom is bugging you to get off the phone; you want to talk to your friends on the phone more.
3. You just told your parent you would mow the lawn this afternoon; your friend is on the phone and wants to go play basketball.
4. You want designer jeans; your parent says they cost too much money.
5. You want to stay out after the game with your friends; your parent wants you to come home right after the game.
6. You want to go to the shopping mall with your friends; your parent says it's not a place to go and hang around.
7. Your family was planning to go to a ball game together; now your friends want you to go with them for pizza.

Part 2—Work with your partner to devise a plan to earn the freedom you want.
1. You want to stay out later during the week; your parents say no.
2. You want to stay overnight at a friend's; your parents say no.
3. You want to go to a party with friends; your parents say no.

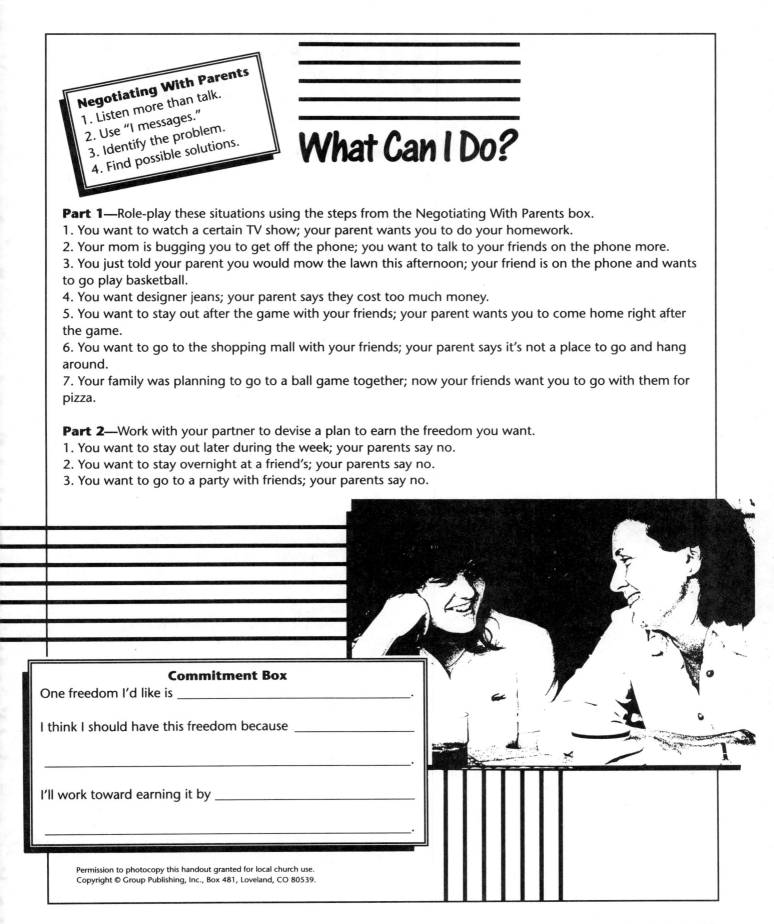

Commitment Box

One freedom I'd like is _____.

I think I should have this freedom because _____

_____.

I'll work toward earning it by _____

_____.

LESSON 4

SHOWING LOVE

I t's easy for junior highers to take their parents for granted and just expect them to be there and provide for them. Here's an opportunity to explore creative and fun ways for kids to express the love they have for their parents.

LESSON AIM

To help junior highers expand their ways of showing love to their parents.

OBJECTIVES

Students will:
- study Jesus' way of loving others;
- discuss ways to show love in everyday situations;
- brainstorm ways to express their love for parents; and
- decide on one new way they'll show love to their parents.

BIBLE BASIS
JOHN 15:12
GALATIANS 5:13b

Look up the following scriptures. Then read the background paragraphs to see how the passages relate to your junior highers or middle schoolers.

In **John 15:12**, Jesus tells his disciples to love each other as he has loved them.

In the verse immediately following this command, Jesus describes the ultimate expression of love: laying down your life for another. Together, these verses describe love as a serious, powerful commitment.

Today love is often portrayed as only sentimental or sexy. Jesus' unselfish, unconditional love toward us is a model for us in showing love to others. By studying how Jesus showed his love for us, junior highers will learn that love goes far beyond feelings. Love is a decision that involves giving of yourself.

In **Galatians 5:13b**, Paul is instructing the Christians about freedom and love.

In Christ we're free—not to do whatever we please or to serve ourselves but to lovingly serve each other. An often overlooked dimension of love is serving.

Middle schoolers don't readily understand serving. But

through this verse, kids can discover how serving their
parents is a way of saying "I love you."

THIS LESSON AT A GLANCE

Section	Minutes	What Students Will Do	Supplies
Opener (Option 1)	5 to 10	**Together**—Draw something they like to do with their parents.	Paper, markers
(Option 2)		**I Like . . .**—Name qualities they like in their parents.	
Action and Reflection	up to 10	**Find a New Way**—Find different ways to express love.	3×5 cards, pencils
Bible Application	10 to 20	**How Jesus Loves Me**—Discuss ways Jesus shows his love for us.	Tape, newsprint, markers, Bibles
Commitment	5 to 10	**How I Show Love**—Evaluate ways we show love to our parents.	Newsprint, markers, bag of Hershey's Kisses, "ABCs of Showing Love" handouts (p. 42), pencils
Closing (Option 1)	up to 5	**Parent Coupon**—Make love coupons for parents.	"Loving Heart Coupons" (p. 43), pencils
(Option 2)		**Circle Prayer**—Pray a prayer of thanks for God's love.	

The Lesson

☐ OPTION 1: TOGETHER

Give kids each a sheet of paper and a marker.

Say: **Draw something you really like to do with your
parents.**

When everyone is finished, have kids each share their
drawing with the group.

Ask:

● **How do you feel when you do this activity with your
parents?** (Comfortable; close.)

● **What'd happen if you told your parents how much
you enjoy doing this with them?** (They'd be surprised; they
already know.)

☐ OPTION 2: I LIKE . . .

Form groups of three. Have kids each complete these

OPENER
(5 to 10 minutes)

statements within their groups:
- Two qualities I like about my mom are . . .
- Two qualities I like about my dad are . . .

Be sensitive to kids from single-parent or blended families. In place of "mom" and "dad," you may substitute "stepmom," "stepdad" or simply "parent" if needed.

Call everyone together, and ask:
- **What'd you share in your groups?** (I like my mom's adventuresome attitude; I like my dad's sense of stability.)
- **How would you feel telling these things to your parents?** (Embarrassed; silly.)

ACTION AND REFLECTION
(up to 10 minutes)

FIND A NEW WAY

Say: **Talking to parents can be tough. It's hard to open up, and it isn't always easy to get your point across.**

Form pairs. Designate one partner in each pair as Siskel and the other as Ebert. Send the Siskels and Eberts to opposite ends of the room to receive their instructions. Give the Siskels each a 3×5 card and a pencil.

Say: **Write a positive, honest message about your partner, such as "You're very giving" or "I like the way you smile." In a few minutes, you'll give it to your partner.**

While the Siskels are writing, go to the Eberts and say: **In a few minutes your partner will come and give you a message. You must sit here and keep your eyes closed. Don't peek.**

Return to the Siskels and say: **Take your message to your partner now. But you may not talk at all.**

After the Siskels deliver their messages, have the Eberts keep their eyes closed.

Ask:
- **What's the problem here?** (They're not getting the message; what's this card for?)
- **How were you feeling while trying to give or receive the message?** (Frustrated; wishing I could see.)

To the Siskels, say: **Find another way to give your message to your partner. You can speak, but the Eberts still can't see.**

After the messages are delivered, ask:
- **How do you feel now that you gave or received the message completely?** (Relieved; surprised at the message.)

Say: **There are different ways to express love and thanks. Sometimes we get into a rut and only do it one way. Today we'll discover new ways to express love to our parents. Let's start by looking at biblical examples of expressing love.**

BIBLE APPLICATION
(10 to 20 minutes)

HOW JESUS LOVES ME

Tape a sheet of newsprint to the wall. On the newsprint, write John 15:12. Leave space to write under the verse.

Say: **Before Jesus died on the cross, he met with his**

disciples one last time to tell them what would happen and to give them instructions. One command he gave is "Love each other as I have loved you." (John 15:12.) **Let's look at some verses to find out different ways Jesus showed his love.**

Form groups of three. Assign groups each one of the following verses. Give kids each a Bible. Have groups each read their verse and write on the newsprint ways Jesus shows love in that verse.

● Matthew 8:2-3 (Jesus gets involved, touches the man and heals him.)

● Matthew 20:29-34 (Jesus asks, "What do you want me to do for you?" and takes a personal interest in the man.)

● Luke 22:32 (Jesus prays for Peter.)

● Luke 23:33-34 (Jesus died on the cross, asking God to forgive people.)

● John 13:3-5 (Jesus washed his disciples' feet.)

● 1 John 3:16 (Jesus died in my place.)

Ask:

● **How do these verses relate to the communication game we played earlier?** (There are many different ways to show love; sometimes it's hard to show love no matter how you try to do it.)

● **How many ways are there to show love?** (An infinite number; too many to count.)

● **How would your life be different if you loved others the same way Jesus did?** (I'd be very popular; I'd feel good about myself.)

Say: **Jesus showed his love in practical, everyday ways. He was faithful, he listened to people and he met their needs. Jesus commands us to love others the way he loves us.**

Ask:

● **How could you express Jesus' kind of love in the following situations?**

1. You're watching your favorite TV show. Your mom comes home with a car full of groceries and has brought in two bags. (Help carry bags in; help unpack groceries; thank Mom for shopping; offer to put food away after the show is over.)

2. Your dad's been out of town several days and is coming home tonight. It's been snowing all day. (Shovel sidewalk; make him a treat; make a welcome-home banner.)

3. Your mom's been really tired and not feeling well the past few days. (Ask her how she's feeling; offer to make supper or do the laundry; ask how you can help.)

4. Your mom's driven you to three activities this week so far. (Thank her; make her a card thanking her; offer to help her with something at home.)

5. Your dad's been working overtime all week and comes home exhausted and crabby. (Thank him for working; serve him a treat; put on music he likes.)

6. You want to wear certain clothes for a special event at school tomorrow but they need to be washed. (Offer to fix supper so Mom can start the laundry; start the laundry and see if Mom needs anything washed; tell her about your special event and ask for her help; wear something else.)

After kids have responded, ask:

● **How would your parents feel if you did any of these things?** (Shocked; loved.)

● **How do your parents know you love them?** (They just do; by how I treat them.)

HOW I SHOW LOVE

Say: **Let's brainstorm ways to express love or thanks to your parents. Any idea is great.**

Form two teams. Give teams each a sheet of newsprint and a marker. Say: **List as many ways as you can to show love to your parents. The team with the most ways listed wins a prize. You have two minutes.**

Some possible responses are "Say I love you," "Say thanks," "Tell them the meal is good," "Give a hug," "Speak kindly," "Do what I'm told," "Help around the house" or "Do something special with them."

After two minutes, tally the responses and award the winning team members each a Hershey's Kiss. Or give the winning team a bag of Kisses—then encourage them to show love by sharing Kisses with the whole class. Review both lists, and congratulate kids on their creativity.

Give kids each an "ABCs of Showing Love" handout (p. 42) and a pencil. Have them each complete the handout alone.

When everyone is finished, ask:

● **What did you learn about yourself by completing this handout?** (I show love in many ways; I haven't thought much about this subject before.)

Say: **Star the three ways you show love most often. Share one with the group.**

After everyone has shared, say: **From all the ideas shared today, write down one new way of showing love to your parents you'll try. Then find a partner and share it with him or her.**

After kids share, have kids each tell their partner one thing they admire about the way he or she expresses love. When pairs are finished, ask for volunteers to repeat to the group the ideas their partners told them.

☐ OPTION 1: PARENT COUPON

Give kids each a "Loving Heart Coupon" (p. 43) and a pencil. Have kids each fill out who it's for, the service offered and the expiration date. Share ideas for coupons to help kids get started. For example, kids might decide to make a homemade

---

COMMITMENT
(5 to 10 minutes)

CLOSING
(up to 5 minutes)

dessert of the parent's choice; help for 30 minutes around the house; or babysit so parents can have a date one evening.

Have kids each read their coupon to the group. Tell kids each to deliver their coupon to the appropriate person as soon as possible. And encourage kids to create more coupons in the next few weeks for other family members.

Close with prayer, thanking God for the unique and creative ways we can express our love to our parents.

☐ OPTION 2: CIRCLE PRAYER

Have kids form a circle. Have each person complete this sentence prayer: "Thanks God, for showing you love me by . . ."

After the last person prays, say: **In Jesus' name, amen.**

If You Still Have Time . . .

Thank-You Notes—Have kids each write a thank-you note to their parents for something specific.

I Feel Loved—Have kids each complete these statements:
- I feel loved when my mom . . .
- I feel loved when my dad . . .
- I feel loved when my parents . . .

Again, be sensitive to kids from single-parent or blended families.

Course Reflection—Form a circle. Ask students to reflect on the past four lessons. Have them take turns completing the following sentences:
- Something I learned in this course was . . .
- If I could tell my friends about this course, I'd say . . .
- Something I'll do differently because of this course is . . .

ABCS OF SHOWING LOVE

Below are many different ways of showing love to parents. Rate yourself on how often you show love in these ways (O=often; S=sometimes; H=hardly ever; N=never).

A ___ I ask my parents how I can help.

B ___ I give my mom flowers.

C ___ I try to understand my parents' viewpoint.

D ___ I thank my parents for their help.

E ___ I do things to help without being asked.

F ___ I talk to my parents about things that interest them.

G ___ I do fun things with my parents.

H ___ I treat my parents the way I want them to treat me.

I ___ I listen to my parents.

J ___ I tell my parents I love them.

K ___ I send notes to my parents (birthdays don't count).

L ___ I spend special time alone with Mom or Dad.

M ___ I pray for my parents.

N ___ I let my parents know they're special to me.

O ___ I speak to my parents with respect.

P ___ I thank God for my parents.

Q ___ I tell my parents I appreciate them.

R ___ I hug my mom or dad.

S ___ I give presents to my parents (besides Christmas and birthdays).

T ___ I thank my parents for cooking our meals.

U ___ I thank my mom or dad for working to support our family.

V ___ I forgive my parents when they make mistakes.

W ___ I celebrate special times with my parents.

X ___ I do something special for my parents for Mothers Day and Fathers Day.

Y ___ I obey the rules my parents set.

Z ___ I spend time doing things with my parents because I want to.

Now score yourself according to how many ways you checked.

● **18 to 26**—Bravo! You really know how to let your parents know you care. Keep it up!

● **9 to 17**—Good work! It sounds like you know how to show love to your parents. But you could stand to do it more often or in a greater variety of ways. Pick three ways you didn't check, and try them this week.

● **0 to 8**—Ouch! You need to work on showing love more. Pick out two new ways to show love each week for the next four weeks, and give them each a try. Find ways that are comfortable for you, and meaningful to you and your parents.

LOVING HEART COUPONS

Photocopy and cut apart these coupons. Make enough so each junior higher can have one.

Especially for _____
This coupon entitles you to _____

_____

_____

Coupon expires _____

Especially for _____
This coupon entitles you to

_____

_____

Coupon expires _____

Especially for _____
This coupon entitles you to _____

_____

_____

Coupon expires _____

Especially for _____
This coupon entitles you to

_____

_____

Coupon expires _____

Especially for _____
This coupon entitles you to _____

_____

_____

Coupon expires _____

Especially for _____
This coupon entitles you to

_____

_____

Coupon expires _____

Especially for _____
This coupon entitles you to _____

_____

_____

Coupon expires _____

Especially for _____
This coupon entitles you to

_____

_____

Coupon expires _____

BONUS IDEAS

Class for Parents—Have a guest speaker address parents of junior highers about kids' top concerns. Ask the speaker to give tips for parents on how to make junior high a positive growth time. This could be a one-night annual event or a class for several weeks. Check out *Parenting Teenagers* and *Parenting Teenagers II* video series (Group Publishing) as possible resources for the class.

Let's Get Talking!—Have a night for junior highers and their parents. Have a facilitator introduce basic communication skills, and give parents and their kids the opportunity to practice with each other. Have parents and kids discuss how using communication tools can change their relationship.

TV Families—Have kids watch one or more family TV programs. See how conversations between parents and kids are portrayed. Are they building up or breaking down each other? Watch a popular family comedy and perhaps an old show such as *Leave It to Beaver*. Compare how the parents and kids interact. How is God's viewpoint different from Hollywood's?

No Talking!—Have a non-verbal night for kids. Have kids come to the church for supper, allowing no talking from the moment they enter the building. Have junior highers each eat in silence, then gather them in a group.
Discuss:
● **How did you feel not being able to talk?**
● **What other ways did you try to communicate?**
Play the What Are You Saying? game on page 45.

Table Talk—Use the "Table Talk" handout (p. 19) as a basis for a parent and kids' meeting. Include fun crowdbreaker activities such as the "I Wonder Who" handout (p. 45). Or check out *Quick Crowdbreakers and Games for Youth Groups* (Group Books) for crowdbreaker ideas. Set aside time for parents to talk with their own teenagers.

Parent Appreciation Night—Have junior highers plan and lead an entire event to honor parents. Have kids make and send invitations, plan the menu, cook the meal, prepare and give parent awards, and make up skits or songs about parents. Encourage kids to make it a time for families to enjoy each other. Have kids also plan a worship time thanking God for their parents.

Word List

- affectionate
- cooperative
- proud
- hopeful
- enthusiastic
- happy

- afraid
- confused
- thoughtful
- discouraged
- interested
- jealous

- angry
- frustrated
- worried
- cautious
- thankful
- undecided

- bored
- selfish
- hurt
- suspicious
- sad
- surprised

What Are You Saying?—Write each of the words in the "Word List" box above on separate 3×5 cards. Shuffle the cards, and give one to each person. Randomly pick two kids to non-verbally act out their feelings or attitudes toward each other at the same time. For example, if one person got the "affectionate" card and the other got the "bored" card, then one would show affection to the other who would act bored. Have the group try to guess what words each pair is acting out.

Family Fun Night—Invite junior highers and their parents for a night of great games. Play volleyball sitting on the floor using a beach ball. Play non-competitive games and relays using family teams. Play The Ungame (Talicor, 190 Arovista Circle, Brea, CA 92621, 714-255-7900)—a non-competitive game that helps people learn more about each other. Have each family team build an ice cream sundae in the shortest possible time.

I Wonder Who—Use the "I Wonder Who" handout (p. 46) for a junior high and parent mixer. Afterward, ask fun questions, such as what musical instruments can be played by people in this group, where people have flown, and what Bible verses are their favorites.

Together Time Retreat—Have a retreat for junior highers and their parents. Give families an opportunity to spend time together—having fun and getting to know each other better. Create a relaxed and positive environment.

Have family teams each prepare a family "coat of arms." Have each family design a family holiday and present it to other retreaters. Let families help plan retreat worship in family teams. Play relays and games in family teams. Be sensitive to single-parent families.

PARTY PLEASERS

RETREAT IDEA

I wonder who...

Find people who can answer true to any of the following statements, and have them sign under the appropriate statements. Junior highers may ask only parents; parents may ask only junior highers. You need only one signature per box.

Never wore braces	Has been to a state or county fair	Has water-skied	Had a pet in grade school
Can speak another language	Had no cavities before age 12	Is the only child in family	Can play a musical instrument
Has flown in an airplane in the past year	Had a first job of babysitting	Can't whistle	Can recite a Bible verse from memory
Went to summer camp as a teenager	Has been in more than 15 states	Moved three or more times before age 12	Has never gone downhill skiing

More from Group's Active Bible Curriculum™
Yes, I want Scripture-based learning that blasts away boredom.

For Senior High

Quantity

_____	207-2	**Counterfeit Religions**
		ISBN 1-55945-207-2 $6.95
_____	202-1	**Getting Along With Parents**
		ISBN 1-55945-202-1 $6.95
_____	208-0	**The Gospel of John: Jesus' Teachings**
		ISBN 1-55945-208-0 $6.95
_____	200-5	**Hazardous to Your Health**
		ISBN 1-55945-200-5 $6.95
_____	203-X	**Is Marriage in Your Future?**
		ISBN 1-55945-203-X $6.95
_____	205-6	**Knowing God's Will**
		ISBN 1-55945-205-6 $6.95
_____	201-3	**School Struggles**
		ISBN 1-55945-201-3 $6.95
_____	206-4	**Sex: A Christian Perspective**
		ISBN 1-55945-206-4 $6.95
_____	204-8	**Your Life as a Disciple**
		ISBN 1-55945-204-8 $6.95

For Junior High/Middle School

Quantity

_____	100-9	**Boosting Self-Esteem**
		ISBN 1-55945-100-9 $6.95
_____	118-1	**Drugs & Drinking**
		ISBN 1-55945-118-1 $6.95
_____	102-5	**Evil and the Occult**
		ISBN 1-55945-102-5 $6.95
_____	108-4	**Is God Unfair?**
		ISBN 1-55945-108-4 $6.95
_____	107-6	**Making Parents Proud**
		ISBN 1-55945-107-6 $6.95
_____	103-3	**Peer Pressure**
		ISBN 1-55945-103-3 $6.95
_____	104-1	**Prayer**
		ISBN 1-55945-104-1 $6.95
_____	101-7	**Today's Music: Good or Bad?**
		ISBN 1-55945-101-7 $6.95
_____	105-X	**What's a Christian?**
		ISBN 1-55945-105-X $6.95

Yes, please send me _____ of Group's Active Bible Curriculum studies at $6.95 each plus $3 postage and handling per order. Colorado residents add 3% sales tax.

03151

□ Check enclosed   □ VISA   □ MasterCard

Credit card # _____

Expires _____

(Please print)

Name _____

Address _____

City _____

State _____ ZIP _____

Daytime phone (____) _____

Take this order form or a photocopy to your favorite Christian bookstore. Or mail to:

Group's Active Bible Curriculum
Box 481 ● Loveland, CO 80539 ● (303) 669-3836

Blast away boredom with these upcoming scripture-based topics.

For Senior High:

- Dating
- Making decisions
- Materialism

- New Age
- Being a servant
- Injustice

- Who is God?
- Music and media
- Faith in tough times

For Junior High:

- Success in school
- Independence
- Body-health

- Miracles
- Relationships: Guys and girls
- Sharing faith

- Handling conflict
- Creation
- The Bible

For more details write:

Group's Active Bible Curriculum
Box 481 ● Loveland, CO 80539 ● 800-747-6060